DEVOTIONS for Preteens No. 1

A DAILY LOOK AT JESUS

Original Title:
QUIET MOMENTS WITH GOD

Mary Lillian Miles

MOODY PRESS

CHICAGO

Copyright ©, 1963, by
THE MOODY BIBLE INSTITUTE
OF CHICAGO

1970 Edition

Printed in the United States of America

Preface

DEVOTIONS FOR PRETEENS is the result of an earnest effort to make the Bible both loved and understood by children, and to provide them with a systematic course of readings which will encourage them to have their own devotional time each day.

The present series covers the life and teachings of Christ as they are given in the four Gospels.

The portions are undated so that the child may not become discouraged if sometimes legitimate reasons hinder him from reading. They are numbered and are to be checked as read.

Special mention is due to Dr. Donald E. Demaray, Professor at Seattle Pacific College, through whose kind encouragement the Bible readings, prepared for my own children, have been revised for the use of others.

THE AUTHOR

Quiet Moments with God

Before beginning each day's portion pray:

> Dear Lord, open my eyes that I may see wonderful things in Your Word, and open my heart to receive Your truth.
>
> Amen.

Close your quiet time with God with a prayer that you may live up to the truth you have learned about in His Word. Ask His blessing and guidance for those you love. Pray for your friends who do not yet know Him.

1

READ LUKE 1:5-14, 16.

Good News for Zacharias

What a shock it gave Zacharias to see an angel standing by the altar! He thought he was all alone in that little room where he went to burn incense while the people were praying in the larger room. But the angel had wonderful news for him. For many years Zacharias and Elisabeth had prayed for a baby boy. Soon their prayers would be answered. And theirs was to be no ordinary baby. The angel said he would bring many sinners to the Lord. Don't you suppose Zacharias was overjoyed? Well, perhaps you are wrong. Tomorrow you'll find out.

A VERSE FOR TODAY:

"Thy prayer is heard" (verse 13).
God always hears my prayers. Sometimes He says "Yes," sometimes "No," and sometimes, "Not now."

2

READ LUKE 1:18-22.

Dumb Because He Doubted

You thought Zacharias would be overjoyed by the news the angel brought him, didn't you! Sad to say, he was like a lot of other people when God tells them something—he just didn't believe it. He was a priest of God and a good man too, but he forgot that *all things are possible with God*. Unbelief is a very black sin in God's sight. Because he doubted, he was to be dumb until baby John was born. How embarrassing when he came out and couldn't speak to the people!

TODAY'S THOUGHT:

God can do ANYTHING but fail.

3

READ LUKE 1:26-33, 38.

A Wonderful Message for Mary

It is six months since the angel Gabriel brought good news to Zacharias. Mary was alone, perhaps praying, when she looked up and saw—an angel! And what strange words he spoke to her. Being a simple, humble girl, it troubled her to be called "favored." She thought there must be some mistake. But no, she was actually to be the mother of the Son of God, Jesus, the King of Israel about whom her Bible told. Mary did not doubt, like Zacharias. She pleased God by believing the angel's words. She said: "I am God's servant. I want His will to be done."

A PRAYER FOR TODAY:

> O God, I believe that You are able to do anything, even though it may seem impossible.

4

READ LUKE 1:46-53.

Mary's Hymn of Praise

Mary just had to tell someone her wonderful news. So she went to visit her cousin Elisabeth, Zacharias' wife. It was there that she sang this lovely song of praise to God for His goodness in choosing her to be the mother of Jesus. How grateful and humble she was. She twice speaks of herself as being of "low degree." She says that God scatters the proud like faded leaves, and sends the rich away empty; but He exalts the humble and fills the hungry with good things.

LET'S SING:

> The birds upon the treetops
> Sing their song;
> The angels chant the chorus
> All day long;
> The flowers in the garden
> Blend their hue,
> So why shouldn't I; why shouldn't you
> Praise Him too.

READ LUKE 1:57-66.   5

The Baby Is Named

The friends and neighbors who came to the house to rejoice over the birth of the new baby were very surprised that he was not to be named after his father. Why did Zacharias name him "John"? (Luke 1:13) I wonder why God didn't want him called Zacharias? Don't you think God gave him a different name so that the parents might always be reminded that he belonged to Him and had a special work to do? God knows *your* name. As soon as Zacharias' tongue was loosened he praised God. No wonder, for God had been better to him than he deserved. In II Timothy 2:13 we read: "If we believe not, yet he abideth faithful." Zacharias found that this is true.

THINK ABOUT THIS:

> Satan puts all kinds of doubts in our minds, but if God has said He will do something, nothing on earth can stop Him.

6

READ LUKE 1:67, 68, 76-80.

Baby John's Father Foretells His Future

The angel had told Zacharias wonderful things about the baby God was going to send him, and now God gave Zacharias another peep into the future. He said John would be called, "The prophet of the Highest." Looking down the years he saw that God in His love and mercy would send Jesus, and His coming would be like the dawn of a new day after a very dark night (verse 78). He would bring light and peace to those who had been in the darkness of sin. John would be a preacher, and would prepare people for the coming of Jesus. When John grew up, in what college did he get his training? You'll find the answer in verse 80.

TODAY'S THOUGHT:

> Jesus came to take the darkness of sin out of your heart and to fill you with His light and peace. Have you let Him in?

READ LUKE 2:1-7.

A King in a Manger

No pretty crib, no dainty clothes, no warm, comfortable bed for baby Jesus, God's Son. Just a bed of straw in a noisy place where people and animals came and went. How *much* God loves us, to send His dear Son into this sinful world to be our Saviour. I love Him too, and want my heart to be a clean place where He is pleased to live, don't you?

A SONG FOR TODAY:

> Thou didst leave Thy throne and Thy kingly crown,
> When Thou camest to earth for me;
> But in Bethlehem's inn was there found no room
> For Thy holy nativity.
> O come to my heart, Lord Jesus,
> There is room in my heart for Thee.

8

READ LUKE 2:8-14.

The Heavenly Choir

No wonder those sleepy shepherds were filled with fear. They were all alone in the darkness, watching those little white mounds—their slumbering sheep. Not a sound broke the silence, and not a light pierced the darkness except for the twinkling stars. Suddenly—a dazzling light, a voice saying, "Don't be afraid." And what a strange message—a baby, Christ, the Lord—lying not in a palace but a manger. Then hundreds of angel voices singing praise to God. How good God was to send the news on that first Christmas morning to a few humble shepherds.

LET'S SING:

> Hark! the herald angels sing,
> Glory to the newborn King;
> Peace on earth and mercy mild;
> God and sinners reconciled.

9

READ LUKE 2:15-20.

Night Visitors

The dazzling light and the heavenly music were gone. The hillside was again dark and silent. The shepherds rubbed their eyes. Had they been dreaming? No! They spoke in hushed, excited voices: "Let us go at once and look for the baby." Isn't that just what you would have done? Over dark roads they hurried to the little town of Bethlehem. Before long they found Him, for they had been told where to look. Of course they told Mary and everyone they met about the light, the angels, and the music. Their hearts were overflowing with joy, and they wanted to share it, just as you like to tell others when you have happy news.

A SONG FOR TODAY:

> Away in a manger,
> No crib for a bed,
> The little Lord Jesus
> Laid down His sweet head.

READ LUKE 2:25-33.

Old Simeon Rejoices

Simeon was a very good man, and all his life he had been eagerly looking for the Christ about whom he read in his Bible. God's Holy Spirit whispered to him that he would see this wonderful child before he died. When Joseph and Mary walked into the temple with Baby Jesus, the Holy Spirit said, "This is the One you have been waiting for." Simeon's words reminded Mary and Joseph that the shepherds had said: "The angels told us this baby is the Saviour, Christ the Lord." They were full of wonder and joy.

THINK ABOUT THIS:

> Jesus' parents took Him to church from the time He was a small baby. Be very thankful if you have Christian parents who take you to church.

READ MATTHEW 2:1-6.

The Guiding Star

The eastern wise men studied the stars and believed that when a very bright star appeared it meant that somewhere a king had been born. This time they were right. Dressed in their gorgeous robes, and carrying costly gifts for the new king, they set out to find Him. When they reached Judea, the land where King Jesus was born, they thought everyone would know about Him and be rejoicing at His birth. They were surprised and disappointed that no one seemed to know about Him. The wicked King Herod was wild with jealousy at the news, and determined to find and kill Him.

THINK ABOUT THIS:

> Herod was troubled at the news of Jesus' birth because he loved his sin and did not want a Saviour. People like the shepherds, who knew they were sinners, rejoiced at His birth.

12

READ MATTHEW 2:7-12.

Wise Men Wonder and Worship

The wise men need not have stirred up such a commotion to find out where Jesus was. They were so afraid that after taking that long journey to find Him, perhaps, after all, they would never see the new king. As they left Jerusalem to go to Bethlehem, expecting a long and difficult search for the baby, they glanced up at the sky. There was the star, shining brightly, just waiting to take them to the very spot! God was watching over His precious Son and He warned the wise men not to tell King Herod where they had found Him.

A COMFORTING THOUGHT:

> God cares for you and me just as He cared for His beloved Son.

READ MATTHEW 2:13, 14, 19-23.

Escape by Night

Baby Jesus had a very special work to do when He grew up. God watched over Him tenderly and would not allow anyone to harm Him. Three times in our portion today He told Joseph in a dream exactly what to do so that the Baby would be safe, and Joseph obeyed at once. These days when we have the whole Bible as our guide, God does not usually tell us what to do by dreams, but He does lead us clearly if we trust and obey. That must have been a very difficult trip in those days when there were no cars, trains or airplanes.

A SONG FOR TODAY:

> Saviour, like a shepherd lead us,
> Much we need Thy tender care;
> In Thy pleasant pastures feed us,
> For our use Thy folds prepare.

READ LUKE 2:40-51.

Lost and Found

What a beautiful picture we have of Jesus in verse 40—a strong body, a wise mind, a clean heart. Jewish boys went to the Temple in Jerusalem for the Passover feast for the first time when they were twelve years old. I wonder what thoughts filled Jesus' mind as He entered His Father's beautiful house. Joseph and Mary looked for Him for three whole days before they realized He was very likely still in God's House. They did not seem to remember that He was different from other children, and would not always be with them.

SOMETHING TO THINK ABOUT:

When Jesus was a boy He loved to go to God's House. Do you?

Read Matthew 3:1-6.

A Strange Looking Preacher

Who was this strange preacher who drew great crowds to hear his message? He didn't spend much money on clothes and food, did he? Nor did he live in a beautiful house on a fine street. There was room for everyone in his church, for it was not a cathedral with comfortable pews and a costly organ— it was the wide open spaces of the Judean country side. John Baptist they called him, because he baptized those who were sorry for their sins. Yes, you are right, he is the son of Zacharias and Elizabeth, grown up now and preparing people for the coming of God's Son.

A VERSE TO MEMORIZE:

> If we confess our sins, He is faithful and just to forgive us our sins (I John 1:9).

READ MATTHEW 3:13-17.

A Voice From the Sky

Although John was telling people about the coming Christ, he didn't know where He was or when He would appear. One day his cousin Jesus came with a crowd of others, asking to be baptized. John had probably often been with Jesus and he knew how pure and sinless He was. He felt unworthy to baptize Him, though he did not realize just then that He was the Christ. But Jesus came to be our example, as well as our Saviour, and He does not ask us to do anything He has not done Himself. The dove and the voice from Heaven made John very sure that Jesus was the Christ, God's Son, about whom he had been preaching.

WHEN YOU PRAY:

> Ask your Heavenly Father to help you to be a joy to Him today. Jesus always pleased His Father.

17

READ MATTHEW 4:1-11.

When Satan Recited Scripture

"This is my beloved Son," God had said when Jesus was baptized. *"If* thou be the Son of God," sneered Satan only a little while later. He knows just when to come whispering doubts and temptations into our ear. Often he comes soon after we have had a good time with the Lord, as we do in Bible Camp or Vacation Bible School. Is it not comforting to know that Jesus was "in all points tempted like as we are, yet without sin" (Hebrews 4:15). Jesus met temptation with the sword of God's Word. See what David said in Psalm 119:11. Are you storing up His Word in your mind and heart?

TRY THIS:

> When you are tempted to do wrong, lift your heart to Jesus, and repeat a Bible verse. Then Satan will leave you.

18

READ JOHN 1:1-12.

Jesus, God's Word

In these verses Jesus is called "the Word" and "the Light." Think for a minute: what are words? They tell what I am thinking about, don't they? And God sent Jesus to tell us that He hates sin but loves sinners. So Jesus is God's "Word" to you and me. He was the true Light too, shining in this dark world. Have you ever received Him as your own personal Saviour? If so, you are a son or a daughter of God. If not, won't you receive Him now? It is just as simple as verse 12 says it is. Read it again very thoughtfully.

A SONG FOR TODAY:

"Into My Heart"

READ JOHN 1:29-34.

Jesus, the Lamb of God

In the long ago days before Jesus came, when a person had done wrong he brought a lamb to the priest. The lamb was killed and the sinner was then forgiven instead of being punished. But an animal could never take away sin! It was a picture of Jesus who would one day die for your sins and mine. That is why John called Jesus the "Lamb of God." Twice in our reading John says he did not know Jesus. He knew Him as his pure and sinless cousin, but he did not know He was the Saviour of the world until after His baptism.

A VERSE TO MEMORIZE:

> Behold the Lamb of God, which taketh away the sin of the world. John 1:29. (Instead of "the world," put your own name there.)

READ JOHN 1:35-42.

Bringing Others to Jesus

Andrew was evidently not a great preacher, for we do not hear much about him in the New Testament, but he brought his brother, Simon (Peter) to Jesus, and Peter was used to bring thousands to the Saviour. I wonder who led Billy Graham to know the Lord? Perhaps some quiet, faithful Christian like Andrew. We're going to get some surprises in Heaven when rewards are given out. Even a child can tell someone about Jesus. Have *you?* Jesus changed Simon's name to Cephas (Peter), meaning "stone." Simon wasn't anything like a stone! He was a weak and cowardly person, but Jesus was going to change him and make him steadfast, like a rock.

THINK ABOUT THIS:

> If you give yourself to Jesus as Peter did, He will change you into the kind of person God wants you to be.

21

READ JOHN 1:43-49.

Come and See

Instead of arguing with Nathanael, Philip said simply, "Come and see for yourself." Anyone can speak a word for Jesus like that. When Nathanael realized that Jesus had seen him as he sat thinking in a quiet place in his garden, and that Jesus had looked right into his mind and heart, he was amazed. Can you see his astonished face as he said, "Teacher, you are the Son of God, and the King of Israel!" We should remember that we are never hidden from the eyes of God.

A VERSE TO MEMORIZE:

Thou God seest me (Genesis 16:13).

22

READ JOHN 2:1-10.

Jesus at a Wedding

Aren't you glad we can ask Jesus to be present at our social times, as well as at our church meetings? Don't be troubled about the way Jesus spoke to His mother. He was not rude or cold in the language of that day. How surprised those servants must have been when Jesus told them to fill the jars with *water*. But they obeyed. And then they looked, and looked again—yes, each jar was full to the brim with rich wine (not the wine of today which makes people drunk). I wonder how long they kept such a secret!

SOMETHING TO REMEMBER:

> In your play time and at your parties, you'll always have a better time if you ask the Lord Jesus to be present.

READ JOHN 3:16-21.

God's Love Gift

We all know John 3:16 by heart. Perhaps we rattle it off so fast that we've never really stopped to think of what it means. Think a minute. God *so* loved you and me and everybody, that He gave the only Son He has, the Lord Jesus Christ, to die on the Cross for our sins. If you, or I, or anyone believes in Him with all our heart, we shall not be shut out forever from Heaven, but we shall live forever and forever with Jesus in His beautiful home. But oh! how important it is to put your faith in Jesus—to trust Him as your Saviour. Read verse 18 again very thoughtfully.

A SONG FOR TODAY:

> Try singing the words of John 3:16 to the tune of "Silent Night," beginning
> John three sixteen,
> John three sixteen,
> For God so loved the world that He . . .

24

READ JOHN 4:5-10.

Tired and Thirsty

It was noon hour; the sun was hot; and **Jesus** was very tired and thirsty. He had purposely traveled through Samaria so that He might help this poor sinful woman. Jews looked down on Samaritans, so the woman was surprised when He spoke kindly to her and asked for a drink. Never before had a Jew spoken courteously to her. But what strange words—"living water" which was "the gift of God." Yes, a drink of water can satisfy our thirsty mouths, but Jesus can satisfy our thirsty souls.

THINK ABOUT THIS:

> When someone offers you a gift, what do you do? Of course you take it and say "Thank you." Have you taken God's gift, the Lord Jesus?

READ JOHN 4:11-15.

Was It Magic Water?

The woman thought He had some magic kind of water that would quench her thirst forever, so she wouldn't have the job of coming to the well every day! Jesus tried to make it clear to her poor sinful heart that He could satisfy fully all the longings of her soul for a better life. He Himself is the living water. It is very hard for unsaved people to understand the Bible, just as it was hard for this sinful woman to understand Jesus' words. If you are not saved the Bible will seem a strange book to you, but when you know Jesus as your Saviour, you will soon learn to understand and love His Word.

A SONG FOR TODAY:

> I am feeding on the living Bread,
> I am drinking at the fountain head,
> And whoso drinketh Jesus said,
> Shall never, never thirst again.

What? never thirst again?
No, never thirst again!
And whoso drinketh Jesus said,
Shall never, never thirst again.

26

READ JOHN 4:25-30.

Good News Travels Fast

Jesus told the woman that He was Christ—the One they were looking for because their Bibles told about His coming. She believed at once because He had told her things about her own life which she thought only a few of her friends knew. Who else but the promised Christ could know all about her, though she had never seen Him before? This news was too good to keep. She forgot that she had come to the well to get water. Leaving her waterpot on the ground, she hurried back to the city to bring her sinful friends to Jesus. She just said, "Come and see." That's simple, isn't it. Have you invited someone to come to Jesus and see how wonderful a Saviour He is?

A POEM FOR TODAY:

> She brought her friends to Jesus
> By simply saying, "Come,
> I've found a Friend who knows me,
> And everything I've done."

If Jesus Christ has saved you,
And filled you with His joy,
I know He counts on you to tell
Some other girl or boy.

27

READ JOHN 4:39-42.

Revival in Sychar

There was a revival in that city because the Samaritan woman believed in Jesus and right away started telling others about Him. Think of the change in that little town when that sinful lady and her wicked friends were saved and their lives completely changed. The cheaters became honest, the liars became truthful, the robbers gave back the things they had stolen, and there was joy and rejoicing on every street. How happy Jesus must have been, for this was why He came, as He said once—"I came not to call the righteous, but sinners to repentance." Verse 39 says that many believed because of her testimony. Has anyone believed because of *yours?*

THINK ABOUT THIS:

> You never know how many lives may be changed if you will speak a word for Jesus whenever you can.

28

READ JOHN 4:46-53.

A Sick Boy Healed

Jesus said, "Go home, your son is better." This was to see if the man really believed in His power. If he hadn't he would have said, "No, no, please come and touch my son and heal him." But that nobleman was in earnest, and he believed with all his heart in Jesus' power. Can't you see him hurrying home to his son, saying over and over to himself, "He's better. I *know* he is." First his servants met him with the good news; and then as he drew near his home, I can just see that boy running out joyfully to meet his father.

TODAY'S THOUGHT:

> You can be quite sure that what Jesus says is always true.

READ LUKE 4:16-22.

A Sermon Worth Hearing

Did you notice that verse 16 tells us it was Jesus' custom (or habit) to go to church on the Sabbath day? I hope it is your custom to go to church and Sunday school on Sunday. It must have been hard for Jesus to preach in the old home town church, because there were many heads together whispering, "It's Joseph's son, isn't it? A carpenter's son preaching? Whoever heard of such a thing." He chose a Bible reading from Isaiah which told of the work He had come to do. What beautiful words—"to preach the gospel to the poor, to heal the brokenhearted, to rescue sinners taken captive by Satan, and to make the blind see."

SOMETHING TO REMEMBER:

> Before you were saved you were a prisoner of Satan. It was Jesus who set you free!

30

READ LUKE 4:23, 24; 28-32.

An Angry Congregation

Imagine people getting up in church and pushing the preacher out! Why were they so mad? Because Jesus had been telling them that whenever a servant of God spoke in his own home town the people would not listen to him. He told them two stories from the Old Testament to show how Elijah, the prophet, was not able to work miracles in his own country. Jesus was preaching now in Nazareth, where he had lived as a boy, and He told His old friends and neighbors plainly that He couldn't do any wonderful things in their city because they did not believe in Him. They didn't let Him finish that sermon!

THINK ABOUT THIS:

It's no use at all asking Jesus to do something, if we do not believe He can do it.

READ MATTHEW 4:18-22.

Four Fishermen for Jesus

You will remember that Simon had already been introduced to Jesus. Each day as he worked at his fishing business he thought about the One who had given him his new name, Peter. How he longed to see Him again! And then one day —could that be Jesus walking slowly along the sandy shore? He stopped and called to Peter— "Follow me." Someone else could have his fish, his boat, his nets—he was off after Jesus *at once*. Have *you* heard His call? Are *you* following Him? Today, fish for a boy or a girl at school— invite him to go with you to Sunday school. Pray for him. You may catch him for Jesus.

A SONG FOR TODAY:

"Fishers of Men"

32

READ MATTHEW 4:23-25.

Sick Bodies and Sick Souls

Did you ever see a huge crowd? I did some years ago when I once saw the King and Queen of England. Thousands of people were crowded around a raised platform where they both stood waving. Jesus was the center of just such a throng of people, all pressing to get closer to Him, especially those who brought sick ones to be healed. Did you notice it says that He healed *every* kind of disease? The list included diseases which even today doctors are not able to cure. Think of the hundreds of sick people who were healed at once by His loving touch.

THINK ABOUT THIS:

> No one was too sick for Jesus to heal, and no one is too sinful for Jesus to save.

33

READ MARK 1:29-34.

Healing Hands

After preaching the morning sermon Jesus went home with Simon and Andrew, but He didn't get any rest! If He had been like some preachers He would have said, "Tell these people to come back tomorrow; I'm too tired to see them tonight." But Jesus never thought of Himself when someone needed Him. Imagine the whole city gathered at the door of Simon Peter's little home! The lame people limped there slowly, the blind were led there, the sick were carried there. Can you see that crowd—babies, boys, girls, men, women, and old folk? Touched by Jesus' healing hands they walked and ran and jumped—perfectly well and strong.

A PRAYER POEM FOR TODAY:

> Healing Hands of Jesus,
> On the sick were laid.
> Boys and girls and grown-ups,
> Well and strong were made.

Healing Hands of Jesus,
Just the same today.
Touch my sinful soul, dear **Lord**,
Cleanse me now, I pray.

34

READ MARK 1:35-39.

Morning Devotions

Jesus must have gone to bed very late and very weary after helping all those sick people who crowded around Peter's door. But long before daylight He got up and tiptoed out of the house. Then away down the deserted, dark streets He walked until He came to a lonely, quiet place. There He knelt to talk with His Father in Heaven and receive new strength for the busy day ahead. Soon He heard voices—they were looking for Him. With new joy and peace and courage He went to His work. If Jesus needed to pray to His Father each morning, so do you and I. Begin each day with a prayer.

THINK ABOUT THIS:

> A good time to have quiet moments with God is first thing in the morning. Your whole day will be happier.

35

READ MARK 1:40-45.

The Unclean Made Clean

"A leper!" screamed someone, and the people standing around Jesus ran away as fast as they could. Leprosy was a terrible disease, and those who had it had to live away from towns, all by themselves. When they saw a well person approaching they had to call out "Unclean, unclean." The leper in our story disobeyed all rules and came right up to Jesus. Instead of looking horrified, and standing as far from him as He could, Jesus actually touched him. Verse 41 says He was "moved with pity." Never to his dying day would that leper forget His face, His touch, His voice. He just couldn't keep silent about Him, but his disobedience made it hard for Jesus because such huge crowds thronged Him.

THINK ABOUT THIS:

> Sin is much more terrible than leprosy. Has Jesus touched your heart and made it clean?

READ LUKE 5:1-11.

Generous Pay

A queer pulpit Jesus had that day—a little boat floating on a blue, blue lake; and the congregation seated on the sandy shore. Simon Peter must have felt so honored to have his dirty little fishing boat used by the Master. And how liberally he was rewarded for lending Jesus his boat. Peter knew that by all the rules of fishing there wasn't a chance for them to catch anything right then, but he obeyed. What happened made him realize that Jesus was most surely God's Son. Those fishermen didn't even stop to sell the fish —they left *all* and followed Him.

TODAY'S THOUGHT:

> No one should ever say to Jesus, as Peter did, "Depart from me." No matter how sinful you feel, Jesus will cleanse you and make you useful.

37

READ MARK 2:1-5.

Four Faithful Friends

Imagine the nerve of those four men! No doubt the crowd outside the house told them, "You might just as well go home. We've been waiting for hours to get in." But where there's a will, there's a way. Using the outside stairs they soon had the sick man on the roof. Quick as a wink they had fastened a rope to the corners of the bed and made a large hole in the roof. I imagine the crowd was speechless with surprise as they saw the stretcher being slowly lowered. Jesus surprised them all by forgiving the sick man's sins before He healed him. A clean heart is far more important than a healthy body.

A VERSE TO LEARN:

Create in me a clean heart, O God (Psalm 51:10).

Read Mark 2:6-12.

In by the Roof; Out by the Door

He couldn't get in by the door; but he got out, bed and all. The astonished crowd made way for him. The scribes were the religious men of that day. They said long prayers and read the Word of God, but alas, their religion was like a robe that covered up black hearts. They hated the Lord Jesus because He was so good and because He could work miracles. In their hearts they grumbled: "This is terrible! Only God can forgive sin. Who does this man think he is!" By healing the man Jesus proved He *was* God.

Think about this:

> Going to church and saying prayers may fool people into thinking we are good, but we can't fool God.

39

READ LUKE 5:27-32.

A Cheater Changed

Tax collectors were known to be expert cheaters. They got rich by overcharging the people and putting the extra in their own pockets. When Levi (known also by the name of Matthew) heard a voice saying, "Follow me," he looked up from his money into the purest and loveliest face he had ever seen. Jesus won his heart. He wanted his gang to know the Master too, so he gave a big dinner for them all. That started the tongues wagging. Jesus, eating with tax collectors—unthinkable. But Jesus said He came for the very purpose of healing sin-sick souls.

A LOVELY POEM TO LEARN:

> I heard His call—come, follow; that was all.
> My gold grew dim;
> My soul went after Him.
> I rose and followed; that was all.
> Who would not follow if he heard Him call?

40

READ JOHN 5:1-9 (a).

The Worst Case at the Pool

The sick people who lay around the pool believed that an angel stirred up the water now and then, and the one who first got into the pool after this, would be healed. The man in our story was partly paralyzed and could move only very slowly. Again and again he had dragged himself painfully to the edge of the pool, only to be bitterly disappointed. Each time someone stepped in ahead of him. Jesus picked him out with His tender, loving eyes, because he was the most hopeless, helpless case there. "Sir, *I have no one,*" he told Jesus—"no one to help me. I shall *never* get better." And the very next moment he was completely well and strong. How wonderful Jesus is!

TODAY'S THOUGHT:

Jesus delights to help when no one else can do anything for us.

41

READ JOHN 5:9 (b) -16.

It Isn't Safe to Sin

In our story today Jesus warns the man He has just healed not to sin any more, or he may become more sick than he was before. So we see sickness is *sometimes* a punishment for wrong doing. But not always: later on (John 9) we shall read about a man born blind. Jesus said neither the blind man nor his parents had sinned. There are several reasons why God allows sickness. I have found that I never feel His presence quite so real and precious as when I am ill; so I can thank Him for times of sickness. Next time you are sick, ask Him to come very near and speak to your heart.

SOMETHING TO REMEMBER:

Sin always brings sadness and suffering.

READ JOHN 5:24-29.

Not Guilty

Let's put verse 24 in our own words: when we believe in the Lord Jesus as our own personal Saviour we no longer face a hopeless death and then God's judgment. Right now all our sins are forgiven and we *have* eternal life. When we close our eyes in death, it will only be that we are finished with this body. Our soul will be free to be forever with the Lord Jesus. The unsaved will live again too—but they will never, never enter God's beautiful Home. Are you certain you will not be with them? Are you *sure* you have passed from death to life?

A VERSE TO MEMORIZE:

> Verily, verily I say unto you, he that heareth my word, and believeth on him that sent me, hath everlasting life (John 5:24).

43

READ MATTHEW 12:9-14.

It's Always Right to Do Good

Does your teacher ever answer your questions by asking you another question? That's what Jesus did here. His question not only answered the Pharisees, but it shut their mouths so they were ashamed to ask any more "catch" questions. Of course they would help a poor sheep out of a hole on the Sabbath day; but heal a sick man—oh, no! That was work. It just shows, doesn't it, that it's possible to be very strict about keeping certain rules, as going to church and not working on Sundays, and yet to have a hard, unloving heart. It's too bad people can get so mixed up in their minds as to think it is a sin to do good.

REMEMBER THIS:

It is never wrong to do good!

READ LUKE 6:12-19.

Helpers Chosen

With what great care Jesus picked His special helpers. All night long He was alone on the mountainside talking with God about it. Then in the morning He chose twelve men from among the large number of His followers. These twelve were called apostles, which means, "sent ones"—sent to help Jesus in His work. How thrilled they must have been to be chosen. They were not great men, or learned men, or saints. Some were fishermen, one was a tax collector—but they were all willing helpers. Would Jesus have chosen you?

A PRAYER FOR TODAY:

> "Here am I, send me." You will find it in Isaiah 6:8. Jesus will let you be His helper if you are willing.

READ MATTHEW 5:1-12.

How to Be Happy

Blessed means happy, so these verses give a recipe for happiness! Verse three needs a little explanation—I think "poor in spirit" means humble, not thinking one's self to be great and important. Jesus says these are happy people because in His Kingdom the truly humble are chosen for places of leadership. The pure in heart are happy too. Sins make your heart impure, and then you are unhappy; so ask God to keep you from sin. Even a little sin can hide God's face. I think verse nine is especially for children. Did you ever stop a quarrel? Try it, and you'll know how happy a peacemaker feels.

A VERSE TO LEARN:

> Blessed are the peacemakers, for they shall be called the children of God (Matthew 5:9).

46

READ MATTHEW 5:13-16.

Where Is Your Light?

How do you like the rolls when mother has forgotten to put the salt in them? Not so good! And if the salt ever became "flat," you might as well throw it out. It wouldn't be any good—neither would a lamp burning away underneath a barrel. And a Christian who doesn't live for Jesus and speak for Jesus is like tasteless salt and a covered light. He is the Light, and if you let Him He will so fill your heart with His joy that your face will shine, and others will want to know Him too.

A SONG FOR TODAY:

"This Little Light of Mine"

47

READ MATTHEW 5:21-24.

Make Up That Quarrel!

Jesus says anger is as bad as murder. Did He really? Well, look again at verses 21 and 22. Next time you begin to feel angry with your brother or sister or any one, think of these solemn words and ask God to take the anger from your heart. Jesus makes it very plain, too, that we must not bring an offering to church if we've had a fight with another Christian. Even if it means leaving in the middle of the service, we must first make up that quarrel. This gives us a very good idea of what Jesus thinks of anger and quarreling.

A VERSE TO LEARN:

> Be ye kind one to another, . . . forgiving one another, even as God for Christ's sake hath forgiven you (Ephesians 4:32).

48

READ MATTHEW 5:34-37.

About Swearing

How plainly Jesus tells us in these verses just what He thinks of swearing. Do you *always* speak the truth; always keep your promise? If so, people will trust your "yes" and "no," and respect you for not using bad language. I once heard of a Christian who heard another man swearing by using the Lord's name in vain. Quietly he said, "Pardon me, but it hurts me to hear you speak that way about my best Friend." If we claim to be followers of Jesus, let's be sure our lips glorify Him.

A PRAYER FOR TODAY:

Set a watch, O Lord, upon my lips.

49

READ MATTHEW 5:38-42.

About "Getting Even"

Did you ever say, "I'll get even with him"? I've even heard Christians say that, and by the look on their faces, they surely meant it! But what does Jesus say? Slap for slap, kick for kick? Oh, no! He says pay back good for evil, kindness for meanness, love for hate. These are the laws of His Kingdom, and if you say you are His follower, He expects you to do what He says. Remember what Jesus said: "Why call ye me Lord, *and do not the things which I say?*"

HOW ABOUT IT?

> Can your friends tell by the way you act that you belong to the Lord Jesus?

50

READ MATTHEW 5:43-48.

How to Treat Your Enemy

Are you a child of God? Jesus spoke these words for *you*: "Love your enemies, do good to those who hate you, pray for those who treat you very badly." *Do* you? If all God's children really did these things our homes and schools and churches would be happier places, and sinners would want to know our Saviour. Anyone can love those who are loving and kind, but it takes a real Christian to love those who hate him, and to be kind to those who are mean to him. Let's begin today.

WHEN YOU PRAY:

Ask God to give you love for that boy or girl who gives you a bad time.

51

READ MATTHEW 6:1-6.

Do It Secretly

When you gave your offering last Sunday, did you let those around you see how much you were giving? Did you drop it noisily on the plate, and then sit back feeling as if you had done God a big favor? If you did, you've had your reward; don't expect any more. Did you pray, or give a testimony in church so that people would think how good you are? If you did, you've had your reward. Let's take these verses to heart and do our good works secretly so that our heavenly Father can reward us.

REMEMBER:

Don't blow your own horn.

52

READ MATTHEW 6:9-15.

Learning to Pray

We can say the Lord's prayer by heart without even thinking. Have you ever said it slowly and thought about what it means? "Hallowed" means blessed or holy. When we come to our Father in prayer we must remember that He **is** holy. "Thy Kingdom come"—one day He will be King over this whole earth. We want that to happen soon, don't we. "Thy will be done in earth"—you'll help to answer that prayer by doing His will today. And don't forget—you're asking Him to forgive you *in so far* or as you forgive others.

WHEN YOU PRAY:

> Don't ask God to forgive your sins until you have first honestly forgiven that girl or boy who was mean to you.

53

READ MATTHEW 6:19-21.

The Bank of Heaven

Have you heard of the rich Christian lady who was very busy making money and buying expensive things? One night she dreamed she was being shown around Heaven. Pointing to a lovely big house the angel said, "This is your gardener's home." She was very surprised, for he was a poor man, but he was always busy serving the Lord. Imagine her feelings when the angel pointed to a little cottage and said, "This is your house, lady." In tears she asked the reason for this, and was told: "We did our best with the materials you sent up."

TODAY'S THOUGHT:

> The time and money we use for ourselves never reach the bank of Heaven. Are you laying up treasures in Heaven by serving Jesus now?

54

READ MATTHEW 6:25-33.

Don't Worry

"Take no thought" means "do not worry about it." It is right to plan carefully for our food and clothes, but very wrong to worry about them. "Your heavenly Father knows"—what comforting words, especially for Mother and Daddy who must provide for the family. And remember, He always keeps His promises: "Seek *first His Kingdom and His righteousness*"—be eager first of all to please Him—and all these things that you need *shall be yours as well.*

A POEM FOR TODAY:

> Said the Robin to the Sparrow: "I should really like to know
> Why these anxious human beings rush about and worry so."
> Said the Sparrow to the Robin: "Friend, I think that it must be
> That they have no heavenly Father such as cares for you and me."
>
> —Elizabeth Cheney

55

READ MATTHEW 7:1-5.

Is There a Log In Your Eye?

Imagine a man with a log in his eye making a fuss about a speck in his brother's eye! Ridiculous, isn't it. But certainly not sillier—or sadder—than the boys or girls who are always finding fault with others, when they themselves have far too many faults. It's so easy to see what's wrong with someone else—but what about yourself? When you're sure there's not a thing wrong with you—*then* you may find fault with someone else. And don't forget, if we're hard on other people, others will be hard on us. We reap exactly what we sow.

A VERSE WORTH REMEMBERING:

> There's so much good in the worst of us,
> And so much bad in the best of us,
> That it hardly behooves any of us
> To talk about the rest of us.

56

READ MATTHEW 7:7-12.

Bread and Fish, Not Stones or Snakes

In these verses Jesus encourages us to pray and expect an answer. But notice what He says: if a child asks for *bread* or *fish* his father will not give him a stone or a snake! He didn't say if the child asked for a gold watch or a TV set he would get it. James says (4:3) "Ye ask and receive not, because ye ask amiss that ye may consume it upon your lusts." This means that if we ask for something just for our selfish enjoyment we will *not* receive it. We find a wonderful rule to live by in verse 12. Next time you are about to do something which you know is not very kind, just ask yourself this question: Would I want him to do that to me?

A VERSE TO MEMORIZE:

Verse 12, which is called The Golden Rule.

57

READ LUKE 6:46-49.

Will Your House Stand the Storm?

You've all watched a house being built. A good builder digs down and puts in a strong concrete foundation so that the house will stand firm in stormy weather. We are building day by day —the house of our own lives. If we not only hear about Jesus, but *do* what He says, we are making a good strong foundation for our lives. Then when storms of temptation and trouble come, we shall not go all to pieces, but will stand firm. If we call Him "Lord," let's do what He tells us.

A SONG FOR TODAY:

> My hope is built on nothing less
> Than Jesus' blood and righteousness;
> I dare not trust the sweetest frame,
> But wholly lean on Jesus' name.
> On Christ, the solid Rock, I stand,
> All other ground is sinking sand.

58

READ LUKE 7:2-10.

A Soldier's Faith

This centurion was a Roman soldier. The Romans had conquered the Jews and were usually rough and cruel, but this man was *kind* and had even built them a church, so evidently he believed in their God. He was *humble* too—he didn't even feel worthy to ask Jesus to heal his servant, nor to have Him in his home. But his Jewish friends who came to Jesus said, "He *is* worthy." Not only was he humble, but he had *great faith,* and his faith was rewarded.

THINK ABOUT THIS:

> It isn't "sissy" to be a Christian. Many great soldiers were followers of Jesus; for one, General MacArthur.

59

READ LUKE 7:11-17.

A Dead Man Comes Alive

It was wonderful for that poor broken-hearted mother that Jesus came to her city just at the right moment. Can you picture the scene—the loud wailing (for women in that country cry loudly), the bowed form of the mother, the stretcher covered with a sheet carried slowly by four men. Then Jesus came—everyone stops, a hush—and in the silence His voice, "Young man, arise." And then—the rejoicing! Jesus doesn't stop funeral processions today, but He has promised that one day we shall be with loved ones again. Oh, what a time of rejoicing that will be!

WORDS OF COMFORT:

> The hour is coming . . . when the dead shall hear the voice of the Son of God, and they that hear shall live (John 5:25).

60

READ MATTHEW 11:28-30.

Work That Doesn't Tire

You may not know yet what it feels like to be very weary, but you've often seen grown-ups completely worn out, and to all such people there are no words in the world more comforting than these: "Come unto me . . . and I will give you rest." The yoke is a bar or frame of wood that joins two oxen so that they walk and plow together. If we work with Jesus, we shall learn to be gentle and humble, and we'll know what it is to have rest and peace in our souls.

JUST TRY IT:

> Let Jesus help you pull your load (your problems and worries). He takes the heavy end.

61

READ LUKE 7:36-39.

A Gift of Love

The Pharisees were proud and very careful to appear religious. But Jesus said it was like making only the outside of a cup clean, while the inside was very dirty. Probably the only difference between this Pharisee in our story and the sinful woman was that *she* humbly confessed her sin, while *he* covered up his! How truly sorry for her sins she must have been to come into his home when she probably thought he would scorn her. But Jesus would not scorn her; He is a true Friend of sinners.

A COMFORTING PROMISE:

> The Lord is nigh unto them that are of a broken heart, and saveth such as be of a contrite spirit ("contrite" means truly sorry) (Psalm 34:18).

62

READ LUKE 7:40-50.

How Much Do YOU Owe?

As Jesus told this story about the two debtors Simon must have felt his face getting redder and redder until he wished the floor would open and let him drop! Notice what Jesus said to the woman— "Your *faith* has saved you." Not "your tears," or, "your loving gift." No, nothing can save our sinful souls except faith in the Lord Jesus. That just means believing with all our hearts that He will forgive us if we are truly sorry for our sins, and ask His pardon. Have you ever heard Him say, "Your faith has saved you; go in peace"?

A THOUGHT FOR TODAY:

F A I T H means
F orsaking
A ll,
I
T ake
H im

63

READ MATTHEW 12:46-50.

Who Are Jesus' Brothers and Sisters?

Of course it was a wonderful thing to be Jesus' mother, or his brother or sister, but in our Bible reading today He says that if you do His will you mean the same to Him as His mother, brothers and sisters. You can see how wrong people are who say we should worship Mary and pray to her. Jesus didn't say, "Make way for Mother Mary, she wishes to speak with me, bow down and pray to her." He said—"You who do my will are my mothers, sisters, brothers."

A SERIOUS QUESTION:

Do you belong to Jesus' family?

64

READ MATTHEW 13:1-9.

A Story About a Farmer

We have ears, but sometimes the very things we ought to listen to go in one ear and out the other! Are you listening? Jesus was a wonderful teller of stories. This story is called a parable. A parable is a story with a special meaning. Most of these people probably got nothing out of it because they didn't stop to think about it. But it sank deeply into the hearts of those who listened carefully and thought about it. I am sure they stayed to hear more.

A HELPFUL HINT:

> When you read God's Word, pray like little Samuel of old, "Speak, Lord, Thy servant heareth."

65

READ MATTHEW 13:18-23.

Is My Heart Good Ground?

Jesus explains His story clearly. The seed is the Gospel message, and the soil is people's hearts. There are four kinds of "soil"—the path, the rocky ground, the thorny ground and the good soil. What is "good soil"? I think it is a heart softened by the Holy Spirit, broken up perhaps by troubles, and ready to welcome the Gospel seed. Only in the good soil does the Gospel seed grow and bear fruit—the fruit of love, joy, peace, kindness, obedience, humility, and other fine things. Are these lovely things growing in your heart?

WHEN YOU PRAY:

> Ask God to take all the hardness out of your heart so that the seed of His Word may take root and grow.

66

READ MATTHEW 13:44-46.

Hidden Treasure

What is the Kingdom of Heaven? It is the place and people under the rule of King Jesus. Right now He rules in the hearts of His own people, but one day He will rule over all the earth. It's good to belong to His Kingdom. Just as the merchant in our story sold all he had to buy one very valuable pearl, so I would have given all I had, if necessary, to become a member of Christ's Kingdom. Those who find Jesus as Saviour, find treasure indeed, worth more than the whole world.

A QUESTION TO THINK ABOUT:

> If you had to give up everything in order to have the Lord Jesus as your Saviour—would you be willing?

67

READ MATTHEW 8:23-27.

Asleep In a Storm

A great storm, a rough wind, waves beating into the little boat—and Jesus asleep! How tired He must have been to sleep through it all. The disciples in the boat had seen Him work many miracles. They had even seen Him raise a dead man to life—and yet they are frantic with fear. They do not realize who He is or they would know that "no [storm] can [destroy] the ship where lies the Master of ocean and earth and skies." This same Jesus brings peace and rest to stormy hearts.

A CHORUS FOR TODAY:

> They all shall sweetly obey My will,
> Peace, be still; peace, be still.

68

Read Matthew 8:28-34.

A City That Begged Jesus to Leave

One word from Jesus, and these two terrible fellows were changed into quiet, sensible men. The evil spirits who had made frightened men of them, completely destroyed a whole herd of pigs. The people saw the two changed men, no longer fierce and wild; they saw the dead bodies of the pigs in the water; and they actually begged Jesus to go away! Their pigs were more important to them than their souls. But their souls will one day appear before God—what good will pigs and money do then? If you had all the money in the world, and did not have Jesus as your Saviour, you would be far worse than poor.

A verse to learn:

> What shall it profit a man if he shall gain the whole world and lose his own soul? (Mark 8:36).

69

READ MARK 5:21-24; 35-43.

Brought Back to Life by His Loving Touch

How understanding and loving the Lord Jesus was. When news came that the little girl was dead, He at once comforted and encouraged the troubled father—"Do not fear, only believe." Then at the home, how His words must have cheered the sorrowing parents—"She is not dead; she is sleeping." That's what Jesus thinks of death. He can just as easily bring a dead person to life as you can waken a sleeping person. He took the little girl's hand in His strong, loving hands. And how kind of Him to remind her mother that she needed something to eat.

A POEM FOR TODAY:

> The sick and sad, the blind and lame,
> Came to God's holy Son;
> No one on earth could make them well—
> He healed them every one!

70

READ LUKE 8:43-48.

A Case the Doctors Had Given Up

Twelve long years she had been sick. Mark tells us she had spent all her money going from one doctor to another, but had become worse instead of better. Can you see her, bent over with weakness, pushing and struggling to get close to Jesus? Just a touch, and at once she knew she was well. Overjoyed, but feeling unworthy, she tried to slip away, but Jesus wanted to assure her that it was her *faith* in His power, and not any magic in His robe, that had healed her. How sweet His words must have sounded in her ears, "Go in peace."

A CHORUS FOR TODAY:

> O touch the hem of His garment,
> And thou too shalt be free;
> His saving power this very hour
> Shall give new life to thee.

71

READ MATTHEW 9:27-33.

The Multitudes Marveled

A little girl brought back to life again; a poor sick lady healed; now two blind men made to see, and a dumb man made to speak! No wonder the people said they had never seen anything like it before. Jesus was careful to tell these sick people that it was faith in His power that brought healing to them. "Do you believe that I am able?" He said. When you ask the Lord Jesus for something you must believe with all your heart that He is able to do it.

DO YOU BELIEVE THIS:

> There is nothing too hard for Jesus;
> There is nothing that He cannot do.

72

READ MARK 6:1-6.

Jealous of Their Neighbor

Jesus got no welcome when He came to the place where He lived as a boy. His friends and neighbors were jealous of His power and wisdom. Wasn't He the carpenter, a member of a family they knew well? How was it that *He* could work wonders? Yes, He was a carpenter, Mary's son, but He was God's Son too. Because they would not believe that, He could not do His mighty works there. It is just as we learned in our last reading, if we ask the Lord Jesus to do something for us, we must believe with all our heart that He is *able* to do it.

THINK THIS OVER:

> Is there something Jesus cannot do for you simply because you don't believe He can?

73

READ MATTHEW 9:36—10:4.

Sheep Without a Shepherd

I have never seen a flock of sheep without a shepherd, but I can imagine that sheep would run hither and thither in utter confusion. A crowd of people looked just like sheep to Jesus. His great heart of love was filled with pity as He saw their worried faces and realized how utterly unable they were to find the way to God and Heaven. He saw them, too, like a field of wheat, ready to be harvested for God, if only there were reapers, and so he chose "apostles" to help him teach these lost people the way home to God.

A SONG FOR TODAY:

> Who'll go and help this Shepherd kind,
> Help Him the wandering lambs to find;
> Who'll bring the lost ones to the fold,
> Where they'll be sheltered from the cold.

74

READ MATTHEW 10:28-33.

Who Cares About a Sparrow?

Do you want Jesus to tell His Father that you are His child? I'm sure you do. Then *you* must have courage to tell your friends that you belong to Jesus (verse 32). Some may laugh at you, but in this country they are not liable to hurt you. But do you know that in some countries people are put in prison and sometimes even killed if they say they are followers of Jesus. The Lord Jesus tells us not to be afraid of those who can only hurt our bodies. The only one to be afraid of is Satan, who not only can destroy a man's body (or a woman's) (by drink and such things), but can drag a soul into Hell. This he can never do to a person who is trusting in Jesus.

A POEM FOR TODAY:

> God loves the flower in the field,
> The sparrow in the tree.
> If He so loves the little things,
> I know He cares for me.

75

READ JOHN 6:4-14.

A Boy Who Shared His Lunch

Andrew was evidently not a great preacher, for we do not hear much about him in the New Testament. In a quiet way he did some things which really counted. One way was to bring his brother Peter to Jesus—Peter who was later used to win thousands to the Saviour! And now we read of his faith in bringing the little boy and his lunch to Jesus. I wonder how the little boy felt. I imagine he never got tired of telling what happened that day. Let us give whatever we have to Him—ourselves, our time, our money, and believe that He will use what we give in His own wonderful way.

TODAY'S THOUGHT:

> You will be amazed at what Jesus can do with the little you have to give Him, but be sure to give Him yourself first.

76

READ MATTHEW 14:22-27.

Can It Be a Ghost?

It is pitch dark—between three and six o'clock in the morning. The wind is blowing so hard and the waves, tipped with white foam, rush at the little boat and toss it about mercilessly. The disciples are already frightened, for they think the boat will upset any minute. Suddenly they see a white shape moving toward them. Someone whispers, "A ghost." They are frozen with fear. Can you imagine their relief when that sweet, familiar voice says, "It is I, be not afraid." Jesus let them battle the storm for awhile, but He didn't come to them too late. He never does!

A VERSE FOR TODAY:

What time I am afraid I will trust in thee (Psalm 56:3).

77

READ MATTHEW 14:28-36.

Peter on the Water, Then in the Water!

So long as Peter kept his eyes on Jesus he was able to walk on the water, but the minute he looked at the waves, down he went. I imagine he might have said to himself: "Well, just imagine *me* walking on the water!" Splash—he began to sink. Or, "Oh, dear, I can't keep this up; I just know I'll sink." . . . "Help, help"— he *was* sinking! We can't live the Christian life in our own strength. If we are proud and depend on ourselves we shall sink in the waves of sin, but if we keep trusting in Jesus we can walk safely through life.

TRY THIS:

> When things are hard, don't look at your troubles and difficulties, look at Jesus.

78

READ JOHN 6:22-29.

Food for the Body, or Food for the Soul

The people wanted to know how Jesus got to the other side of the lake, but what they wanted most of all was another good feed like the picnic they had from the boy's lunch. Jesus' words fed their souls, but they would rather have food for their bodies. People will work so hard to get bread and butter to keep their bodies alive, but food and bodies do not last forever. Our souls do. So we should be eager for spiritual food which is God's Word so that our souls may be fed.

ASK YOURSELF:

> Am I starving my soul?
> A good meal each day on God's Word will keep it healthy and strong.

79

READ JOHN 6:35-40.

How to Live Forever

Some parts of the Bible are hard to understand, but nothing could be simpler than verse 40. It is a promise we can count on absolutely, because it is made by One who *never* breaks His Word. So if you have seen the Lord Jesus in the pages of God's Word, and have believed in Him with all your heart, you *have* everlasting life (life which lasts forever and ever). If you have not yet believed in Him as your own Saviour, verse 37 is the one for you. "Him that cometh to me I will *in no wise cast out.*" This includes you and also the greatest sinner living!

A POEM FOR TODAY:

> Children can in Him believe,
> Children can His grace receive;
> None He ever has cast out,
> I will not His kindness doubt.

80

READ JOHN 6:66-71.

Many Turn Back; Few Follow Faithfully

Verse 60 says: "After *this* many drew back and no longer went with Him." After what? It was after He had spoken to them of things they couldn't understand because they did not *want* to understand. Instead of coming and asking Jesus to explain, they probably said something like: "This is too deep for me; let's go home and forget about Jesus." How foolish! Sadly Jesus turned to His own twelve helpers and said, "Are you going to leave me too?" Aren't you glad Peter said what he did, out of a heart full of love for His Lord?

A PRAYER FOR TODAY:

> Lord, I won't leave you. You have taught me about eternal life.

81

READ MATTHEW 15:29-31.

People Were Simply Amazed!

Can you picture Jesus sitting on the grassy hillside looking out over the blue waters of the Sea of Galilee, a great crowd of sick people lying on the grass near Him, hundreds more walking slowly up the winding path? There is a boy helping a lame man, and there is a mother leading her little blind girl. Some are carried on the backs of others; some carried on stretchers. "And He healed them." Those are such simple words. What shouts of joy must have resounded as lame people leaped, the blind saw and the dumb spoke. Don't you wish you had been there?

A SONG FOR TODAY:

> Tell me the stories of Jesus,
> I love to hear,
> Things I would ask Him to tell me,
> If He were here.
> Scenes by the wayside,
> Tales by the sea,
> Stories of Jesus,
> Tell them to me.

82

READ MARK 7:32-37.

"Astonished Beyond Measure"

No wonder they were astonished. This man didn't jabber any more. And they didn't have to shout at him—he could hear as well as anyone. Sometimes Jesus just spoke a word, and the sick one was healed at once; but sometimes He touched the blind eyes or the deaf ears; and sometimes He even put something on them. He *can* heal us at once in answer to prayer, but He *does* use medicine and doctors. We should ask Him to bless the means used, and not forget to thank Him when we have recovered. He asked them not to tell about the healing of the dumb man because it would bring still greater crowds.

REMEMBER THIS:

> The Lord Jesus is the best doctor. He may want you to use medicine, but be sure to ask Him about it.

83

READ MARK 8:1-9.

A Three-Day Conference Without Meals

I wonder how many of us would stay for three days listening to the Word of God without food! How kind and thoughtful Jesus was. He not only fed their souls, but He thought of their need for food. They had brought no food, but He wouldn't let them go home hungry. His disciples had seen Him feed five thousand people with five loaves and two fish. Why were they so stupid as to doubt that He could do it again! Jesus gave thanks for the food. Is this done in your home? If not, why not do it at the next meal. If the family does not wish to join in the prayer, give thanks silently. At home, at school, in restaurants, this is one way you can quietly witness for your Lord.

A PRAYER TO SAY AT MEALTIME:

> Thank You for the world so sweet,
> Thank You for the food we eat,
> Thank You for the birds that sing—
> Thank You, God, for everything.

84

READ MARK 8:22-26.

Walking Trees

A day or two ago in our reading we noticed that Jesus did not always give immediate healing. It is even clearer in today's story that healing is not always given right away. Don't you think it was a test of the blind man's faith when his sight was only partly restored—he saw, but people looked like trees! He was not discouraged, for he knew Jesus would heal him. Let us learn to wait, and pray, "Thy will be done."

A PRAYER FOR TODAY:

O Lord, give us patience when You don't answer our prayer right away. Help us to trust and wait.

85

READ LUKE 9:18-22.

What Would You Have Said?

John the Baptist, the man who preached about the coming of Jesus, the "Lamb of God," was dead. Some of the people thought Jesus was John come to life again, and some thought He was Elijah come to life again. Jesus' own followers knew that He was God's Son, the Christ whose coming was told about in their Old Testament Scriptures. They wanted everyone to know and to crown Him King, but Jesus explained that He *must* first suffer and die. Why? Because we are all sinners, and only by His death on the Cross could He save us.

AN IMPORTANT QUESTION:

> Whom do you say Jesus is? Can you honestly say, "He is my Saviour"?

86

READ LUKE 9:23-26.

How to Lose Yourself

This reading sounds like a lesson in arithmetic, doesn't it. What do we mean by the cross that we are to take up daily? We remember that the cross was something on which a person died. Jesus wants the selfish, mean, unloving, sinful *me* to die every day, so that we may live new lives, full of His love, joy, peace, and all that made His life so beautiful. That's what it is to deny ourselves and lose our lives.

A POEM FOR TODAY:

> The loss of gold is great;
> The loss of time is more;
> But losing Christ is such a loss
> That nothing can restore.

87

READ LUKE 9:28-36.

The Voice from the Cloud

Peter, James, and John were special friends of Jesus, perhaps because they loved Him more than the others did. They never forgot the wonderful sight which they saw on the mountain that day. Peter speaks of it in his letter years later—I Peter 1:16-18. Jesus, Moses, and Elijah spoke of "His departure which He was to accomplish at Jerusalem"—this meant His death on the cross for our sins. Peter was one of those blundering people who speak without thinking. He was so thrilled he wanted to stay on the mountain forever! God's voice from the cloud silenced him—"This is my beloved Son, listen to *Him.*"

A HINT FOR HAPPINESS:

> God's Word advises us to be swift to hear and slow to speak. Most of us should talk less and listen more.

88

READ LUKE 9:37-43 (a).

A Difficult Case

When you hear the word "majesty" what do you think? Beautiful snow-capped mountains, kings in their royal robes, mighty rivers flowing toward the ocean? When Jesus healed the poor boy in our story, "They were all astonished at the majesty of God" (A.S.V.). He is more powerful, more beautiful, more majestic than earth's mightiest king. It was sad that Jesus came down from that wonderful time on the mountain to find that His disciples had failed to help this boy. How disappointed He was when He said, "How *long* am I to be with you and bear with you?" He told them later that they failed because they did not really believe in God's power, and because they did not pray.

TODAY'S THOUGHT:

> Your minister may disappoint you, and your Sunday school teacher may fail to help you, but "Jesus never fails."

89

READ LUKE 9:43 (b) -45; MATTHEW 17:22, 23.

Born to Die

The Lord Jesus came to this earth to die for our sins. We do not know how old He was when He realized that He must die on the cross one day, but He knew it and thought of it often while He healed and taught the people. From time to time He told His disciples that He must one day be killed by wicked people. They could not understand it, because He was so popular wherever He went. Verse 43 (b) tells us that they were all marveling at everything He did! Crowds often change very quickly, and it was not long before some of these same people were shouting, "Crucify Him!"

A THOUGHT FOR TODAY:

> The Lord Jesus came into this world to die for you and me. What wonderful love!

90

READ MATTHEW 17:24-27.

A Fish That Paid the Tax

Peter was embarrassed by the question, "Does your Teacher pay the tax?" He said "Yes" out of love and loyalty to Jesus. I think I see him walking quickly away in case anyone questioned further. With a troubled heart he enters the house where Jesus is—he hates to ask the Lord about it. But Jesus has read his thoughts. What a relief when Jesus brings up the subject. It was a temple tax, and Jesus, God's Son, certainly did not have to pay it. How kind and understanding He is—lest the tax collector should not understand, and lest Peter be troubled—He had arranged a surprise fish. In its mouth was the exact tax money needed for two people!

A HYMN FOR TODAY:

> My Father is rich in houses and lands,
> He holdeth the wealth of the world in His hands;
> Of rubies and diamonds, of silver and gold,
> His coffers are full—He has riches untold!

91

READ MATTHEW 18:1-6.

How God Measures Greatness

Jesus called a little child. He was not afraid to go to Jesus, even if he was surrounded by big people. With Jesus' loving arms around him, he was perfectly happy. Those wise looking men learned a lesson from the child—they must be humble, loving, eager to learn, trustful—like children. He told them that if they received a child lovingly it was just as good as kindness done to Himself, and anyone who caused a little child to fall into sin deserved to be drowned! How very *much* He loves children.

A HYMN FOR TODAY:

> Jesus loves me, this I know,
> For the Bible tells me so.
> Little ones to Him belong,
> They are weak, but He is strong.

92

READ MATTHEW 18:10-14.

Little Lost Lambs

The shepherd searches long and earnestly for little lost lambs. Jesus, the good Shepherd, is sad if one little child is wandering away from Him. He loves His sheep and lambs so much that He died for them on the Cross. If you haven't yet come to His loving arms, He is searching for *you*. And if you are His, is it not wonderful to know that there are angels in Heaven whose duty it is to watch over you. Let us be careful not to grieve our loving Shepherd by disobeying Him and wandering into sin.

A VERSE TO MEMORIZE:

> I am the good shepherd: the good shepherd giveth his life for the sheep (John 10:11).

93

READ MATTHEW 18:21-27.

How Many Is 70 x 7?

How often have you asked God to forgive you? We could never begin to count all the sins He has forgiven, could we. And yet we find it hard to forgive a sister, brother or friend for even *one* sin against us. Peter thought the Lord would think he was very forgiving when he suggested that he should forgive his brother seven times. I think he got a shock when he heard the answer —70 times 7! That makes 490 times—which is the same as saying, "Forgive him every single time he sins against you." Are we obeying the Lord Jesus in this matter?

A PRAYER FOR TODAY:

> O heavenly Father, help me to be kind, tender-hearted, forgiving—even as you have forgiven me for Christ's sake.

94

READ MATTHEW 18:28-35.

A Man That Didn't Practice the Golden Rule

We read in the last portion about the servant whose debt of thousands of dollars had been freely forgiven by his master. Imagine this same fellow seizing by the throat a man who owed him only $20.00 and demanding that he pay him immediately. It's unbelievable, isn't it! And yet we are just as bad if we do not forgive someone who wrongs us, when God has forgiven *all* our sins. And there's a serious warning here. Jesus says we will *not* be forgiven if we do not forgive others *from our hearts*. It's easy to say "Oh, I'll forgive you this time," but God looks into our hearts and knows if we really mean it.

REMEMBER THIS:

> If you have a grudge in your heart against someone, it's no use asking God to forgive your sins.

95

READ JOHN 8:12-20.

Don't Walk In the Dark

Once when I was a little girl we arrived at our summer home late at night and had to walk down a very dark trail through a forest without a light. It was not a pleasant experience, and I was very glad when we came out of the dark woods and saw the lights of our cabin. To walk through this world without Jesus is like walking through a dark forest. But when we take Him as our Saviour and follow Him, it is like walking in beautiful sunlight; for He is the light of the world. I hope you are not stumbling along in the darkness without Jesus. If you are, read verse 12 again and let Jesus, the light of the world, flood your heart with His light and love.

A VERSE TO MEMORIZE:

> I am the light of the world: he that followeth me shall not walk in darkness, but shall have the light of life (John 8:12).

96

READ LUKE 9:51-56.

Don't "Pay Back"

Jesus doesn't force people to receive Him. He does not push the door open. He stands and knocks—you may open and welcome Him, or you may leave Him outside. But James and John loved Him dearly and could not bear to have Him treated rudely. They knew, too, that He was the Son of God, the Messiah, and they felt everyone should receive Him gladly. Jesus taught them that His followers must never try to "get even." They must have forgotten what He once told them on a hillside: "Do good to them that hate you, . . . pray for them that despitefully use you." (Luke 6:27, 28, A.S.V).

TODAY'S THOUGHT:

> Paul speaks of the "meekness and gentleness of Christ." If His Spirit dwells within us, we too will be humble and gentle.

97

READ LUKE 9:57-62.

A Dangerous Little Word

What an important little word "but" is. Three men in our story tried to fool themselves into thinking they were willing to follow Jesus—*but*. I think Jesus knew the first man liked a comfortable place to stay, and that is why Jesus told him that He had no home. The second man wanted to stay at home until his father was dead—then he would follow. The third man wanted to go home first to say good-by. Jesus knew that man would let his friends persuade him to stay at home. When you make up your mind to follow Jesus, be sure you have no *buts*—I will, *but*—in your promise.

A SERIOUS QUESTION:

> When you decided to follow the Lord Jesus, did you really mean it? An Indian Christian wrote: "I have decided to follow Jesus—no turning back."

98

READ LUKE 10:1-6; 19, 20.

Lambs Among Wolves

The seventy helpers were to have no money with which to feed and clothe themselves, nor any weapon with which to defend themselves. They were like lambs among wolves; yet they were given great power over Satan and his wicked spirits. God was on their side, and nothing at all could hurt them. Jesus told them not to get excited over this, but to be filled with joy because their names were written in Heaven. Is yours? Revelation 21:27 tells us that the book where their names are written is called the "book of life," and those whose names are found there will enter the gate of Heaven. If you have trusted Jesus as your Saviour, your name is certainly written there. It is something to rejoice over, isn't it!

A SONG FOR TODAY:

> Is my name written there,
> On the page white and fair,

In the book of Thy Kingdom,
Is my name written there?

YOU GIVE THE ANSWER.

99

READ LUKE 10:25-28.

A Catch Question That Didn't Catch

This lawyer found someone far more clever than himself. Probably the Pharisees were standing there, just waiting to see Jesus tripped up. They were always trying to make Him say something against the law, because then they would have a serious charge against Him. How clever He was to make the lawyer answer his own question. Everyone knows that no one can love God as fully as His law requires; nor can we love our neighbor as ourself. We need first to have our sinful natures changed. That is just why Jesus came to die for your sins and for my sins.

A QUESTION ANSWERED:

> What must I do to be saved? . . .
> Believe on the Lord Jesus Christ, and thou shalt be saved (Acts 16:31).

100

READ LUKE 10:29-37.

A Real Neighbor

You shall "love . . . your neighbor as yourself." The lawyer squirmed inside over that part, and hoping to quiet his conscience said, "Who is my neighbor?" (verse 29). He hoped Jesus would say his neighbor was his good friend, the wealthy person he entertained in his home. But oh, no! Once again (verse 37) he answered his own question—the good neighbor was the hated Samaritan (Jews hated Samaritans). If we say we are followers of Jesus, let us be sure we are loving and helpful to all in need, regardless of the color of their faces or the shabbiness of their clothes.

A PRAYER FOR TODAY:

> O Lord, help me this day to be kind and helpful to old people and little children, to the sick, the lonely and the sad, for Jesus' sake. Amen.

101

READ LUKE 10:38-42.

Meddlesome Martha

Martha was all bustle and hurry, eager to have a very special dinner for Jesus. Imagine her grumbling to herself in the kitchen: *"That Mary, there she sits listening to the Master while I do all the work."* Soon she could stand it no longer. She spoke to Jesus. Do you think He accepts service done for Him in a bad spirit? Gently Jesus quieted Martha. He appreciated all that was done for Him, but He was pleased with Mary for realizing that food for the soul was more important than food for the body.

A HINT FOR HAPPINESS:

> You'll serve the Lord Jesus much better if you take time *first* to read His Word and pray.

102

READ JOHN 9:1-7.

Born Blind

Imagine seeing the world for the first time! I wonder where he went first after receiving his sight. Perhaps home to see what his father and mother looked like, and after that I think he went in search of Jesus. How simple was Jesus' command—"Go, wash in the pool of Siloam." The blind man might have said, "I don't know how to get there; water's dirty—I don't want to wash there; it isn't necessary, just make me see now." If he had argued like that he would have been blind for the rest of his life probably. Some people try to tell God how they want to be saved, but He has said, "Believe on the Lord Jesus Christ and thou shalt be saved." If we do not obey this command, we shall never be saved.

A SERIOUS QUESTION:

Have you obeyed God's command: "Believe on the Lord Jesus Christ"? If you have, with all your heart, then you are saved.

103

READ JOHN 9:8-12.

A New Man

"Is not this he that sat and begged?" No wonder they were not quite sure it was the same man! You have seen that hopeless look on a blind beggar's face. Now his face shone and his eyes sparkled. His neighbors and friends asked what had made the great change in him. He answered simply and truthfully. We call that answer "a testimony." Has your life been so changed by Jesus so that your friends will want to know the reason? And do you tell them simply and fearlessly that Jesus has saved you and filled your heart with peace and joy?

A SONG FOR TODAY:

> Come to the light, 'tis shining for thee,
> Sweetly the light has dawned upon me.
> Once I was blind, but now I can see—
> The light of the world is Jesus.

104

READ JOHN 9:13-17.

Cruel Criticism

The Pharisees were supposed to be very religious. They were continually doing things to make people think how very good they were, yet inside they were proud and unloving. They were eager to catch the Lord Jesus doing something wrong because they were jealous of Him. They knew that He was pure and good; they were hypocrites. Imagine saying Jesus could not have come from God because He healed a man on the Sabbath day! They said that was working on God's day. Again the "blind man" gave his testimony simply and bravely.

WHEN YOU PRAY:

> Ask God to give you courage to stand up for Jesus, even though you may be one against a crowd. Just think of what He has done for you.

105

READ JOHN 9:18-23.

Afraid to Speak Out for Jesus

The religious leaders were so bitter against Jesus that they said, "If anyone says He is the Christ, the one foretold about in the Scriptures, we'll not allow him to set foot in the synagogue (the temple, or church)." That was very serious punishment. It meant that you would have no friends and you would be thought as bad as a robber or a murderer. The blind man's father and mother knew that Jesus had opened their son's eyes, but they were afraid of being laughed at; afraid of being put out of the synagogue. Are there times when I don't speak up for Jesus because I'm afraid of being laughed at?

A SONG FOR TODAY:

> Dare to be a Daniel,
> Dare to stand alone,
> Dare to have a purpose firm,
> Dare to make it known.

106

READ JOHN 9:24-29.

Now I See

"We know that this man is a sinner," said the Jews. And yet Jesus had done nothing but good; they could not point to one wrong thing in His life. They were jealous of His power and afraid of Him because they knew He could look into their wicked hearts. Didn't our "blind man" give a splendid testimony—"I don't know a great deal," he said, "but I know one thing and that is that I was once blind and now I can see." When someone wants to argue with you about the Bible just say, "I can't answer all your questions, but I *do* know this—I was once a sinner, but Jesus has saved me and filled my heart with peace."

A TESTIMONY IN SONG:

> Happy day, happy day,
> When Jesus washed my sins away.
> He taught me how to watch and pray,
> And live rejoicing every day.
> Happy day, happy day,
> When Jesus washed my sins away.

107

READ JOHN 9:30-38.

Jesus Found Him

I imagine our friend was feeling a little sad and lonely—cast out of the temple, perhaps even scolded by his parents; *but* Jesus soon found him. He was ready to believe that Jesus was God's Son. Already he loved Him, and with a full and happy heart he bowed his head and worshiped Him. Jesus knew how cleverly and boldly he had stood up for Him against all those dignified religious leaders.

A SERIOUS QUESTION:

> Have you met Jesus face to face, and have you said with all your heart—"Lord, I believe"? If not, say it now—and mean it!

108

READ JOHN 10:1-6.

The Voice the Sheep Know

Jesus is the Shepherd. Grown-up Christians are the sheep, and His children are the lambs. He knows you by your name. When we read His Word we hear His voice. Do you know His voice? Often when we are about to do wrong it is just as though someone tried to stop us—this, too, is our Shepherd Jesus. He does not drive us and push us to do right, but He leads the way, and He calls us to follow .

A HINT FOR HAPPINESS:

> Learn not only to know the sweet voice of your Shepherd, but to obey Him.

109

READ JOHN 10:7-15.

Have You Entered by the Door?

A hireling is paid to look after the sheep and since they are not his own, he doesn't care much what happens to them. But the Shepherd owns the sheep, and loves each one. Jesus, the Good Shepherd, died for His sheep; that helps us to understand how greatly He loves us. He says He came that we might have life, and have it abundantly—a full, happy, satisfying life here on earth, and a Home in Heaven forever and ever. That is far, far better than the hollow pleasures of the world.

A CHORUS FOR TODAY:

> I am the door, I am the door,
> By Me if any man enter in—
> He shall be saved; he shall be saved—
> He shall be saved.
>   (*Action*—Alfred B. Smith)

110

READ JOHN 10:16-21.

Can a Devil Open Blind Eyes?

How terrible that these people let Satan use their tongues to say such awful things against the Lord Jesus. Finally they nailed Him to the Cross. Yet, unless He had allowed it, they would have had no power at all to harm Him. He says in verse 18 that He is going to lay down His life on His own accord for His sheep and lambs. He speaks of "other sheep" whom He is going to bring into His fold. This means you and me and all those who are not Jews—"one fold, and one shepherd." I'm glad He thought of us, aren't you!

TODAY'S THOUGHT:

> This Shepherd so kind had me in His mind, When He laid down His life for His sheep.

111

READ JOHN 10:22-31.

Perfectly Safe

I would hate to be in the shoes of those people to whom Jesus said, "You do not belong to my sheep." How wonderful to be safe in His fold, held securely in His mighty hand, protected by the heavenly Father from all who would like to destroy us. Twice in these verses He says that no one is able to snatch us out of His hand or His Father's. With hearts full of love and gratitude to such a Saviour, let us determine to follow Him more closely than ever before.

A CHORUS FOR TODAY:

> Under His wings, under His wings,
> Who from His love can sever?
> Under His wings my soul shall abide,
> Safely abide forever.
> (*Joyful Melodies*, Newton Jones)

112

Read Luke 11:33-36.

Where Is Your Light?

These are very interesting verses about a candle, or lamp. Another translation of verse 34 reads, "Your eye is the lamp of your body." When our eyes are "sound," or healthy, our whole body is full of light, but if our eyes are not healthy, our body is full of darkness. So it is with our spiritual lives—one little sin can black out our light; so let us ask God to keep our hearts clean so that we may shine brightly for Him. And remember, lamps are not to be put down in the cellar or under a barrel; they are to shine where everybody can see their light.

A hymn for today:

> Jesus bids us shine with a clear, pure light;
> Like a little candle burning in the night.
> In this world of darkness, so we must shine—
> You in your small corner, and I in mine.

113

READ LUKE 12:1-3.

Be Careful What You Whisper

Have you ever watched your mother make bread? She puts the yeast into the center of the flour, covers it over with more flour, and then kneads the dough thoroughly. You can't see the yeast, but soon that lump of dough doubles its size. Leaven is yeast, and Jesus said the hypocrisy of the Pharisees was like leaven. Hypocrisy is pretending to be what we are not. Soon this hypocrisy had made them look like big men! But Jesus warned that though it was hidden from people's eyes, it would one day show up, and everyone would know what very small, mean men they really were. Would you like the things you have only whispered about to be shouted from the housetop or shown on the TV screen? We need to be careful what we *say,* and what we pretend to be.

How about it?

Would you like your friends to know what you are thinking about at all times? Remember, God knows.

114

READ LUKE 12:6-9.

The God of the Sparrows

It should make us have courage to speak up for the Lord Jesus when we think that one day, before all the bright angels, He will say: "This is my child." It is sometimes hard to witness for Him, because no one likes to be laughed at, but when we are with Him in Heaven, oh, how we shall wish we had been more faithful. With God on our side, we need not be afraid of anyone. He who watched over the tiny sparrows says, *"Fear not,* you are worth more than many sparrows."

A POEM FOR TODAY:

> Ashamed of Jesus, that dear Friend
> On whom my hopes of Heaven depend?
> No, when I blush be this my shame,
> That I no more revere (reverence and
>   love) His Name.

115

READ LUKE 12:15-21.

A Rich Man Who Found He Was Poor

Most of us are busy these days from morning until night. What are we busy at? Is it all laying up treasures for ourselves, or do we spend some part of each day or each week giving time and strength to God's work? Many Christians are working far too hard just to get more money, more clothes, a bigger house, a finer car. We shall have to answer to God one day about this. If we are *not* Christians, and things are all we ever think about, we are indeed foolish, like the rich man in our story. We never know when death may come. We must all prepare for it, even though we may be young and strong.

TODAY'S THOUGHT:

> If I am not storing up treasures in Heaven,
> I am far worse off than a beggar.

116

READ LUKE 12:35-40.

Are You Ready?

When you are expecting your mother or father home after a long absence, do you sit around in old clothes, reading a book, the house untidy, dishes not washed, beds not made? No, you put on your good clothes, tidy the house and get a nice meal ready. Then you watch at the window until you see them! Some day Jesus is coming back; it may be today, it may be tonight. Let's be very careful not to go anywhere or do anything we would be ashamed of if He came. He said that He would come when we least expect Him, so we must *be ready!*

A VERSE TO LEARN:

> Be ye therefore ready also; for the Son of man cometh at an hour when ye think not (Luke 12:40).

For a continuation of this series on the life and teachings of Christ as given in the four Gospels, see Devotions for Preteens No. 2.